The Art of Sponsorship
A Course
For Parks, Outdoor Facilities and Non-Profits Serving the Public
By Robert Villegas

The Art of Sponsorship – a Course – For Parks, Outdoor Facilities and Non-Profits Serving the Public
By Robert Villegas

©Copyright 2016 by Robert Villegas – All Rights Reserved. No part of this book can be reproduced in any manner without written consent of the copyright holder or his representative/s.

Published in USA by
Document Services International

ISBN-13: 978-1537185415

ISBN-10: 1537185411

Table of Contents

INTRODUCTION 4
SWOT ANALYSIS 9
DEVELOP YOUR SPONSORSHIP INVENTORY 23
How Does Your Proposal Look? **25**
SPONSORSHIP SALES MATRIX 26
Getting Started **42**
SPONSORSHIP PROPOSAL 45
PROSPECTING – TARGETING POTENTIAL SPONSORS 46
Prospecting Tips **53**
Phone Techniques **56**
Sample Cold Call Phone Contact Script **60**
THE SALES PROCESS 65
THE SPONSORSHIP SALES CYCLE 73
SPONSORSHIP RELATIONSHIP CYCLE 78
SAMPLE SPONSOR PROFILE DATA SHEET 80
Sponsor Profile Data Sheet **80**
CONCLUSION 83
RESOURCES 84
About Document Services International **84**
DSI SPONSORSHIP PROPOSAL SERVICE PACKAGES FOR SPORTS TEAMS, ATHLETES AND ENTERTAINMENT EVENT PROMOTERS 85

Introduction

This short book is based upon my book Finding Sponsors for Sport and Entertainment. It is also based upon a course that I taught for an organization managing Indiana Parks and Recreation facilities. It is, in a sense, a condensation of information from the book geared toward organizations that would like to offer corporate sponsorships on their facilities to help earn revenues.

Robert Villegas
8/19/2016

The Art of Sponsorship

for Parks, Outdoor Facilities and Non-profits serving the Public

Presented by
Robert Villegas
CEO
Document Services International

If your organization depends upon sponsorship, you should understand one thing: The sponsor is the most important element of your success. Sponsors do not serve you; you serve them. The sponsor provides the operating capital and in return is allowed to use your property, community interest and media coverage (within your guidelines) to its advantage.

A company involved in sponsorship of properties like yours get its message across to thousands of potential customers, generates good will in the community, and most importantly, increases market-share and profits. Make no mistake about it, sponsorship is a marketing play, a way to make more money by getting more people to buy products or services.

In general, there are three basic types of sponsors:

1) Primary sponsors have the most visible presence and provide major dollars. They purchase primary logo placement on conspicuous locations throughout an event. They make it a practice of getting the most for their considerable investments by developing additional promotional and hospitality programs. They are the big boys.

2) Secondary level sponsors purchase secondary status at well-traveled but less conspicuous places. These companies obtain smaller signage to make their presence known which helps them maintain or grow their company image. They spend less than the big boys but they are big in their own markets.

3) Associate level sponsors are often smaller companies or, again, large companies where success in their industry requires at least some presence at events or locales such as yours. Such sponsors get involved to enhance a portion of their marketing program. They do not spend as much as the big boys, but still gain more than the cost of their investments. Associate level sponsors can also be brands that accompany a group of other brands in a cooperative marketing program. Sometimes this level of sponsorship prefers to provide product in trade so they can chalk up the investment as a sale while the sponsored organization then sells the products through their own channels.

Sponsorship can consist of more than just signage. A sponsor can access a variety or a combination of sponsorship opportunities such as:

1. Title Sponsorship
2. Official Sponsor
3. Marketing Rights - Licensing Agreements
4. Official Suppliers Rights
5. Driver/Team/Series Sponsor
6. Endorsement Agreements
7. Single Day or Event Sponsorship
8. Broadcast Sponsorship
9. Racetrack venues for sponsors are opportunities to gain name and brand recognition through a variety of means such as:
   - Racetrack signage
   - Contests
   - Product giveaways
     - Cross-promotional opportunities with the team on television, radio, the Internet and at the track.
   - Event Program advertising
   - Hospitality opportunities.
10. Licensing and merchandising rights

Course Outline

Scope
- The Steps
    - SWOT Analysis
    - Develop Inventory
    - Sponsorship Sales Matrix
    - Sponsorship Proposal
    - Targeting
    - Sales Process
    - Sponsorship Sales Cycle
    - Sponsorship Relationship Cycle
    - Resources

SWOT Analysis

SWOT Analysis
- Strengths
- Weaknesses
- Opportunities
- Threats

SWOT Analysis

THE STRENGTHS, WEAKNESSES, OPPORTUNITIES AND THREATS ANALYSIS

One thing few companies do today is conduct a strengths, weaknesses, opportunities, and threats (SWOT) analysis on their company or on any specific aspect of their business especially their sponsorship efforts. Yet, regular and consistent analyses of this type can be critical to future success. A SWOT Analysis is an objective look at the internal elements of your organization, as well as the outside issues that impact your success or lack thereof. If done diligently, you will always have a handle on what you need to do to improve season after season. At the very least, this analysis should be done at the end of each season (or after each event) for both your competitive activities and your sponsorship efforts.

By analyzing and understanding the internal resources available in planning your sponsor search activities, you will gain a better understanding of what you need to do to take advantage of strengths and how to overcome weaknesses. Understanding and planning for both opportunities and threats will give you crucial information for assessing external situations that impact your business, local communities and the sport or entertainment genre you work in.

Needless to say, before you conduct your SWOT analysis, you must become familiar with every detail of sponsorship opportunities and weaknesses in your organization, including budget, personnel, volunteers, time, schedule, series target audiences, and population sizes of the communities where events take place. If you are not, then enlist the time and expertise of the individual you have delegated to perform your sponsor search activities.

Strengths

What distinct competencies does your organization bring to the sport or musical genre? Is there anything unique about you that gives you an advantage you can exploit that would give you an edge, or as Penske would say, to give you the unfair advantage? What additional competencies are possessed by your key employees that might give you an advantage? Consider education, special skills, advanced knowledge? What other resources within the community can you identify that will strengthen your market position? Do you have significant support in the local area, a fan club, great sponsors, large local corporations?

Consider both technical (competitive) skills and marketing skills that you and your employees have developed in previous positions or the experience of organizing and managing a company. The combination of skills, education, along with a knowledge and interest in the sport, certainly provides you with strengths that can help you succeed both in the venue and in the boardroom.

Identify the practical skills and abilities that you or others in your organization may possess. (See Figure 1) Keep in mind, this is not rocket science. Just get a general idea of these skills but also be as specific as you can be. You don't have to take two months to do this. You just want to identify the strengths of your organization. It should only take a few minutes. You can add other things that you come up with at a later time.

Outside Strengths

Needless to say, you have to convince sponsors to support you, so your outside strengths should be well-travelled paths with lots of drive through or walking paths. For instance, tents provided by sponsors can be erected to protect visitors and invite them to visit your sponsors. Or, if they are willing to help the sponsor for a fee. If you need help doing a hospitality event for your sponsor, you can always consult my booklet, Hospitality Event Planning Handbook which you can find on Amazon or at http://amzn.to/2aXiWf8.

Strengths Analysis Checklist – Figure 1

Assess each skill by writing the term strong, average, or weak in the Assessment column.

Skill	Assessment
Financial Planning Budgeting, accounting, management	
Human Resource Management Recruiting, training, supervising, motivating staff and volunteers	
Safety, Security, Risk Management Admissions, venue grounds, spectators, players, personnel	
Hospitality Invitation design and production, amenities, coordination of logistics, hosting activities	
Food and Beverage Negotiations, quality, quantity, contract and price	
Sales and Marketing Prospecting, selling, closing, servicing	
Writing	

Correspondence, promotional copy, internal memoranda, newsletters, trade publication articles, media releases, follow-ups
Leadership Ability
Leadership Ability
Persuasion, motivation, listening, problem-solving skills
Other skills or strengths:

Location Strengths – Analyze each of the following from the standpoint of the location

Strength	Assessment
Capital	
Staff Time to Assist Teams	
Assist in Financial Transactions and Promotions	
Legal Assistance	
Concessions Policies	
Other Strengths (if any)	

Notes and Comments

Weaknesses
Analyzing weaknesses, though not an entertaining activity, is vital to your success. Harmful internal weaknesses can negatively impact your sponsor search program. Convene a meeting with key staff and volunteers to determine any weaknesses that are important enough to address. Ask them to suggest internal areas that are inadequate, that may be controlled and/or corrected, or that should be eliminated before they erode your profitability. Elimination of weaknesses may mean personnel changes, retraining or reassignment, possibly even termination of some people and hiring someone with special skills. Weaknesses and dealing with them are as important to your organization as are strengths because they are the negatives that are drawing you down.

One weakness to seriously look at: Is your marketing program good enough to get you the sponsorship you need?

Use Figure 2 for identifying weaknesses of your property or team.

The Weakness Analysis Checklist - Figure 2
Weaknesses Checklist

Assess each weakness by writing the term critical, controllable, or eliminate in the assessment column.

Weakness	Assessment
Disagreements among key staff and/or volunteers	
Personality conflicts among staff and/or volunteers	
Lack of trained, experienced personnel and/or volunteers	
Short planning time	
Funding problems	
Facility shortage or inadequacies	
Sponsor search	
Other weaknesses:	

Solutions and Action Plans

This approach of assessing your strengths and weaknesses will help you improve your organization and enable you to handle the opportunities and threats from both inside and outside sources. If you don't know what is wrong, you don't know how to fix it. If you don't know your strengths, you don't know how to exploit them. This is what I call focused management and it is much better than just plodding along, don't you think?

Opportunities
The opportunities that present themselves may increase your revenues, but what are these opportunities, how can you recognize them, anticipate them, plan for them?

- Organizational opportunities – What does the organization or association you belong to do for you? Many of them have very effective programs to help you find sponsorship if you offer to promote them in return. Many of them have relationships with beverage vendors, service providers and large corporate clients who use facilities like yours, etc.

- Local Opportunities – Your local area has a strong base of businesses with which you can develop strong relationships – find out how to meet the necessary people and where to hang out so you can meet the Who's Who in local influence. All good people to know. As I mentioned above, a good place to start is your local golf club. One executive I knew years ago told me he got lots of his clients by sitting at the bar one or two nights a week. You might be surprised who you might meet there and at other places where people gather. Don't forget social networking sites. I've had lots of my Facebook friends turn into clients because I sometimes posted some of the work we had done for other clients. You can create your own social media network by setting up a Facebook page and/or Twitter account specifically for your organization. Use proximity locators so that your Facebook friends are notified when they are close to you. Post live video when something great happens and let everyone know your live. Don't forget local business groups such as Kiwanis, Toastmasters and others where you can meet intelligent and industrious people intent on self-improvement and making good connections. Your local Chamber of Commerce and other like-organizations as well would love to keep informed about what you are doing. Or you can look them up on the Internet.

- Event Opportunities – Every event you hold for a customer is an opportunity to sell them sponsorship. Are you ready for these opportunities? Do you have a plan to pursue them and take advantage of them?

Use Figure 3 to identify the opportunities for your team and racing series.

Qualify all opportunities as hot (action required), green (investigate further), lukewarm (possible but not immediate need). Finally, determine whether an opportunity requires action on your part to make it happen.

The Opportunities Analysis Checklist - Figure 3
Opportunities Analysis Checklist

Assess each opportunity for its value by writing the term hot (action required), green (investigate further), lukewarm (possible but not immediate need) in the assessment column.

Opportunity	Assessment
Each Event	
Trade Shows	
Local Events	
Prospective Sponsors	
Associations	
Other (See below)	

The opportunities you identify should each support your goals and objectives. If one does not *entirely* support your end result, determine ways to control it. For example, a tourist-related activity such as a major music festival may be scheduled on the same date as your concert or sporting event. Control this activity to the best of your ability by giving your local fans and sponsors something special that day so they come to your event rather than the festival. Or have flyers passed out at the festival telling people about your event to see how many decide to do both. If they present the flyer at a place of your designation, give them a freebie for coming. Otherwise, this scheduling conflict could become a threat rather than an opportunity.

Threats
Threats of all types may jeopardize the success of your sponsorship efforts. By recognizing potential threats, you gain the advantage of planning ahead.

To determine the range of threats to your success, bring together all organization members for a threat analysis meeting. This includes risk management, volunteers, marketing people and all other critical people. Ask each of them to list any potential threats within their area of responsibility and identify any threats that may affect the organization as a whole. I've always told my people, if you give me a problem, bring the solution with you. That will help motivate them to make a contribution. See Figure 4.

The Threats Analysis Checklist Figure 4

Threats	Comments (Serious – Monitor Further – Requires Coverage or Action)
Personnel	
Business Processes	
Sponsor Search	
Rules and Regulations	
Association	
Other Threats:	

Now that you've finished your SWOT Analysis, enlist your team in a project that will assign an action, a completion date and a "report-back" date for each initiative you will assign to them. Keep record of all this and set schedule items for yourself to follow up to gage how things are going. Remember, we are assessing the impact on your sponsorship efforts, so keep to the topic. But if you discover something else in another area, you should act on that as well.

Develop Your Sponsorship Inventory

Most companies work hard to develop an inventory of promotional programs and opportunities in order to implement their marketing strategies. You should do the same for your organization and for your sponsors. This inventory is basically your little black bag of things that you can do for a sponsor and you should have them on the tip of your tongue at all times. You've already done a lot of work in this area with your Sponsorship Sales Matrix. Now is the time to put that work to use for your proposal. Below are some suggestions on what you can offer your sponsors. These are just a starting point. If you have other ideas, don't hesitate to
offer them to your sponsors.

- Preferred Supplier Status – this status tells the public that you use only this sponsor's products because of your loyalty and their quality.
- Naming Rights – the sponsor purchases the right to change the name of your team or organization so it is no longer the name you gave it but the sponsor's name.
- Official Product Status – similar to Preferred Supplier Status except that you have designated your sponsor as your "official" supplier – this status is most often used for major events like the Super Bowl or Indy 500 or NASCAR, but if your organization garners enough attention, you can do it as well.

- Primary Sponsor – this is the sponsor that obtains primary signage positioning most visible to the public - the primary sponsor provides the biggest share of your budget.
- Secondary Sponsor – the company that purchases a secondary sponsorship obtains logo and/or signage placement visible to the public much smaller than that of the primary sponsor
- Affiliate Sponsor – this company has purchased a smaller signage position or has traded products or services in return for that placement.
- Category exclusivity – this means the sponsor gains exclusive status in a particular industry or product category – they are your only sponsor among their competitors.
- Licensing – this enables the sponsor to be the sole licensee for any products that relate to your organization, t-shirts, posters, etc.
- Endorsements – this is a specific category of opportunity where your team, driver or celebrity endorses a particular product to the public in return for dollars.
- Cross-promotional sponsorship – this is where one of your sponsors gives you product instead of dollars – you take the product and negotiate with another sponsor for special shelf space positioning and advertising in a retail location – then you receive a percentage of the profits from the retailer.

- Customized proposal option – as you will see, it is important that your proposal be flexible. In your proposal, you will offer defined sponsorship packages but you'll also offer the sponsor an opportunity to customize a package that is specifically intended to meet their important marketing goals.

How Does Your Proposal Look?

Let's face it, the "big boys" know how to create attractive proposals. You must ensure that yours is at least as well written and speaks the right marketing language. A neat looking document that presents its subject in a clear and concise manner will get attention regardless of whether it comes in a pretty package. If you struggle with the written word, don't hesitate to ask those around you for editorial and grammatical advice. You don't want to spoil your chances because of a misspelled word or poorly written prose.

Yet with today's computer technologies, color printers and word processing software, it is possible to format your document so it is appealing. If you are not good with computers, ask someone around you to help in formatting and organizing it for you. Just remember, the important issue is whether it is clearly written, well organized and communicates well the benefits of your sponsorship packages. Pay attention to the details of what you are communicating and you will take a big step toward earning sponsorship.

An excellent resource is your local UPS Store or Kinko's. This company has state-of-the-art computers and printers. They can even consult with you on how to make your document attractive, how to properly bind it, cover it and ship it. Take advantage of this low-cost resource to improve the quality of your documents.

Sponsorship Sales Matrix

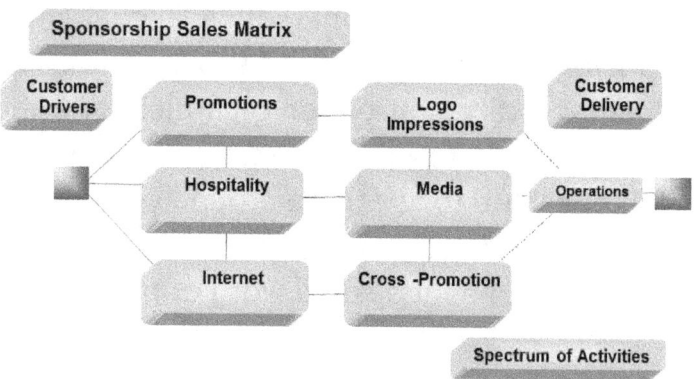

Inventory of Opportunities
- Sponsorship Sales Matrix

This chapter is designed to provide a new paradigm for *organizing* and *selling* sponsorship. These principles apply to all forms of sport and entertainment. The intent and goal of the paradigm presented here is two-fold:

1. It allows you to assist the sponsor in positioning the sponsorship offering based upon his/her key drivers and marketing goals rather than the goal of merely providing sponsorship dollars to your organization, and

2. It focuses you and/or your event around its key purpose which is to provide a vehicle for the promotion and/or sales of brands, companies and products. The result should be a better funded organization.

You might wonder why I say that your key purpose is to provide a vehicle for the promotion and/or sales of brands, companies and products. I think you should recognize that without that specific purpose, without making your organization into a marketing-focused company, you will never be able to do what you love to do which is serve the public and/or make a profit. Sponsors know their marketing goals and as long as you are flying blind about *your* goals, you will never be able to keep your sponsors.

As we will see, we will depart from the traditional development of "sponsorship packages" by adding a "sales cycle" approach that makes you a true marketing partner who understands that sponsorship money is really about sponsorship success – for the sponsor. It can only be this.

The traditional approach has always been about creating some sponsorship packages that list benefits that a potential sponsor can select in order to tell you how you fit in with his marketing goal. I think this basic approach should be used as a starting point for the more important task of working with the sponsor to customize a sponsorship package that specifically meets a sponsors marketing goals, helps him/her address his specific market and grows his business.

In the next two chapters we'll identify your marketing assets and then help you tailor those assets to what you know (through your research) about a potential sponsors marketing objectives. This approach will make you a "perfect fit" for the sponsor and enable you to develop long-term relationships with some highly targeted clients who will come to you because they know you can perform.

Organizing

Developing an effective sponsorship proposal can be a daunting task, especially for the small team or Entertainment Company. The Sponsorship Sales Matrix provides a framework that will allow you to envision and develop your sponsorship inventory. You can use it to organize your sponsorship offerings so they are clear to you and eventually, clear to the sponsor. Each piece of the matrix is a separate category that matches the specific goals of the sponsor to a program that you create for him so both you and the sponsor can see at a glance what it is that you offer and how best to focus upon it. When you put together your sponsorship proposal for a given client, and after having discussed your matrix with him, you will know how to skew your presentation to his/her particular goals.

Selling

The Sponsorship Sales Matrix can also be an effective tool for both selling and up selling your sponsor. The matrix is designed as an "easy-to-remember" package that organizes your sponsorship offerings in a specific order so you can move through the matrix as you discuss the sponsorship with your potential partner. For instance, let's assume your sponsor signed on as an associate sponsor and you tailored your proposal and agreement to the price and range of services that he/she selected. However, if your agreement tended towards a focus on one particular area, let's say, logo impressions, you may later want to direct him toward additional involvement with your web site where you can increase logo impressions significantly by linking your site to his/web site and/or developing special web-based promotions that will draw more traffic to his/her web site. By up selling, later, you can develop an addendum to your sponsorship agreement and gain additional sponsorship dollars. In fact, though the sponsor might be an associate sponsor in one area of your sponsorship matrix that does not mean he cannot pay "primary" sponsorship dollars for an effective program in another area of your matrix. The same could occur, for instance, with a sponsor who is heavily into hospitality and asks you how to increase logo presence at hospitality events that you put on for him/her. The Sponsorship Sales Matrix is a handy tool for starting, developing and improving your sponsorship involvement among your clients.

These are the benefits of the Sponsorship Sales Matrix:

- Your sponsorship offerings are well organized and defined
- They are easy for the sponsor to understand
- You know you can afford them
- You know how to price them so…
- You know how much you have for racing
- You have an effective cross-selling and up selling framework that means…
- You make more money from sponsors

Inventory

Inventory of Opportunities
- Promotions

> **Promotions**
>
> Projects that
> · Sell Products
> · Promote Logos and Brands
> · Action-oriented

To deliver services in the area of Promotions, you will need the following:
- Programs
- People
- Equipment

Programs consist of a number of specific offerings that require people and organization to implement. You have trained marketing people, a relationship with a modelling agency and a set of "promotions" that you can deliver to the customer to promote the company and its products. Equipment may consist of tents, tables, show car, etc., all of which are available to help you deliver the programs that the sponsor needs.

Inventory

Inventory of Opportunities

- Logo Impressions

Logo Impressions

Brand/Logo Identity Strategy
Vehicles
Employee Uniforms
Facility Naming Rights
Website Banners
Web Cam
Merchandising/Freebies/Literature

In the area of Logo Impressions, you will need the following

- Logo or Branding Strategy (worked out with the sponsor in advance)
- Painter or logo Designer

- Print, Media and Video strategies for logo and branding impressions
- Logo Producing Events
- Logo tracking reports over time

By sitting down and developing an impressions strategy with your sponsor, you can develop an effective plan for ensuring maximum logo exposure for his/her products and or brands. Effective delivery of logo stickers and/or banners by your designer will ensure new logos get placed on time and at the right events. You can report your successes to the sponsor after major events or create a monthly report so they see how their signage is doing.

Logo Impressions	# of Events / Days	# of Impressions per season
Brand/Logo Identity Strategy Sponsor Banners and Signage		
Trailer/Vehicles		
Uniforms		
Shop		
Website		
In-car Cam		
Merchandising/Freebies/Hero cards		
Wings on Race Cars		
Driver/Team using		

product		
Other Logo Impressions Below		

Inventory

Inventory of Opportunities
- Hospitality

> **Hospitality**
>
> Logos on Tickets
> Gourmet cooking/meals
> Suites and Tents
> Park Rides
> Tour/travel packages

For Hospitality Events, you will need the following:

- Hospitality Event Planning with the Sponsor – for employees or targeted customer base – best customers to improve business, etc.
- Hospitality Tent/s or Suites
- Gourmet Cook
- Servers and Greeters
- Cooking Equipment and Accessories
- Hospitality and Trackside or Pit Tour Plans and Tour Guides

- Relationship with Ticket Agency and/or Travel Agency
- Limo and/or Transportation Services
- Hospitality Event Planning Workbook (available on Amazon by Document Services International)

Hospitality can be as simple as free passes for 2 people and/or as extensive as major events with lunch, freebies and meetings at the facility. By offering a range of services and prices in this area, you give the sponsor an opportunity to fit everything into his sponsorship budget and, most importantly, you need to be able to price according to what it will cost so there is some mark up for you.

Inventory

Inventory of Opportunities
- Media

Media

News Conference
Press Releases
Press Package
Communications Materials
Newsletters
Television/Radio
Articles

For Media offerings, you need the following

- Media personality contact information – mailing list of media organizations
- Good media relationships
- Employees trained on how to handle media for the sponsor
- Writer for newsletters, press packages, articles, new releases and other forms of communication
- Press representative to look for ways to get your organization and sponsors into the limelight – set up interviews, make sure everyone is where they are supposed to be and ensure the proper "mentions" and "thanks" to sponsors are made

Your price for these services is dependent upon the sponsor's budget, so don't offer more than you can deliver for the amount the sponsor invests. Can one person wear several hats or do you need to be the marketing person to cut costs? Keep in mind a good marketing person here could also be looking for other sponsors.

Inventory

Inventory of Opportunities
- Internet

> **Internet**
>
> Logo link to Web site
> Social Media – FB, Twitter, Instagram
> Proximity Marketing
> Sponsor profile/logo on Web site
> Product sales
> Lead development
> Internet Promotions

For the Internet, you need the following

- A great web site
- A web designer and data base manager who can provide the bells and whistles that make the site exciting and the promotions work
- A logo strategy worked out with the client
- Internet promotions worked out with the client
- Excellent Search Engine Optimization Strategy (SEO) to ensure your site gets visited
- A marketing program to promote the web site on the track, on your literature and everywhere else possible
- A Facebook Page for the organization

- A Twitter Account
- Other Social Media Accounts

Some sponsors may not want Internet presence for the dollars they spend. They may elect to spend dollars on hospitality or logo impression strategies. But later, in conversation, you may be able to get him to sit down with you, once he/she learns of how many hits and potential logo impressions your web strategy is getting for other sponsors – up sell him on the ROI here and you get more money.

Also, become proficient at setting up events in Facebook, using live video, proximity marketing and advertising promotional opportunities on Facebook

Inventory

Inventory of Opportunities
- Cross-promotions

> **Cross-promotions**
>
> Liaison between sponsors
> Cross-promotional product sales
> B2B lead development and liaison

For Cross-promotional offerings, you will need the following

- Creativity
- Flexibility
- Marketing Implementation Manager (You?)

I've long advocated that every sport team should develop a Value Added Program for their sponsors by creating an "association" among their sponsors (and even sponsors of other teams) to develop cross-promotions, B2B transactions and long-term relationships with discount prices among fellow sponsors. You may be able to craft some programs among sponsors where your team retains a portion of the profits to put back into the team – in return for your promotional and/or logo impression assistance. An effective effort here, means the sponsor pays virtually nothing for the sponsorship compared to ROI (and that is the goal after all), and learns to love you as well. In fact, the cost to you is virtually nil but the return in terms of long-term relationships could be incredible.

Sponsorship Proposal

Sponsorship Proposal

- **Sponsorship Proposal**
  - A legal document
  - Thorough explanation of the sponsorship opportunity
    - Marketing value
    - Sponsorship Programs
  - Benefits
  - Prices
- **Proposal Brief**
- **Property Valuation**

Before you get started on your sponsorship proposal, you must understand that you are competing against the "Big Boys." They use professional printing companies, fancy folders, graphic designers, professional marketing writers, cloth letterhead paper and advanced computers and printers. They put their best foot forward to potential sponsors and know how to impress. They even use the power of trackside hospitality suites and Lear Jets. The good news is that you don't need to spend big bucks developing your sponsorship package and you can develop a proposal that looks professional. By putting some thought and effort into your proposal package you *can* compete effectively with the big boys. It doesn't have to cost more than the sponsorship dollars you need and you don't need to hire a consultant who costs more than the team.

The people looking at your proposal are trained professional marketing people who know, for the most part, how to get the most from their marketing programs. They look for professionalism and marketing savvy in the teams they bring on, not just a statement of intentions. This means that if you are going to be successful, your proposal must look like and speak the language of the "Big Boys."

This chapter is written with the small-budget race team in mind. However, the ideas presented here can benefit any sport team and entertainment group including the big-budget organization. Most of these guidelines were developed out of my own efforts to write effective sponsorship proposals for clients.

Getting Started

The first thing to do is set a goal for your document. First, decide how much you will need in order to accomplish your goals. The old Penske axiom applies here: "Speed costs money – how fast do you want to go?" This is your money goal and you should make sure it is an adequate amount. Secondly, you should include in your money goal enough for the time and effort it will take to deliver on the benefits you promise your sponsors. Remember, sponsors are not going to go away once they write the check. They are going to come around to bask in the glory...they expect to be treated well and they want lunch and premium tickets – free. So include these costs as well...and while you are at it, consider money for the people who will do the work of schmoozing the sponsors. They must be paid.

Another key issue before you start is to identify each sponsor's expectations for a sponsorship proposal. Active major sponsors will often produce "sponsorship guidelines" that communicate to teams what they expect to see in the proposal. You should ask specifically if they have such guidelines before you even begin putting something together for them. If they don't have guidelines, here are some important questions to ask your potential sponsor:

- Is our form of public service a category of sponsorship you favor? If the answer is "No," then inquire about

the reason for that. If the reason appears insurmountable, ask what it would take for them to change their mind. Too much resistance here is an indication that you should move on to another potential sponsor. If the resistance is minimal and there is a chance that they would change their minds, then ask if you can include an argument on this in your presentation to them.
- Do you require exclusivity in your industry category? This means, if they are a beer company, they don't want another beer manufacturer on the car or at the event. You will waste your time presenting a proposal if you already have a sponsor competing with them in their industry.
- What is your primary goal in sponsorship and what do you expect to include in their proposal that would reflect that goal?
- Do you require any audience statistical reporting, research or other sales activities at the track or venue?
- Do you look for a certain percentage of the sponsorship investment to be spent by the team on enhancing the sponsorship?
- How much do you usually spend, in addition to the sponsorship investment, in leveraging the sponsorship and what would you like the team to do to support these expenditures? This can be measured in dollars or in a percentage of the cost of the sponsorship (Typically, a sponsor won't get their money's worth unless they spend an equal amount to the amount spent on the sponsorship in leveraging it with additional promotion programs).

- What are your core branding goals? What tag lines, images, icons, values and messages do you seek to promote through sponsorship and how can we aid you in communicating them?
- What kind of cross-promotional strategies have you successfully pursued in the past?

Needless to say, the value of having these questions answered before the preparation of the sponsorship proposal is crucial to the success of your proposal document. A key point to remember, the success of your proposal will depend on how thorough you are in gathering information about your potential sponsor. Most of the time, you won't be able to get this information without their assistance.

Sponsorship Proposal

Sponsorship Proposal Sections

- Executive Summary
- Profile of Organization
- Profile of Opportunity
- Demographics
- Sponsorship Opportunity
- Marketing Opportunities
- Sponsorship Packages
- Sponsorship Benefits
- Contact Information

Targeting Sponsors

- Targeting – Corporate Profile Record
    - www.hoovers.com
    - Demographics
    - Target Markets
    - Sponsor Qualification (how to research a potential sponsor)
    - Strategy development
- SPIN Selling – Selling Solutions
- Traditional Selling
- Becoming a Partner

Prospecting – Targeting Potential Sponsors

Planning which companies you will approach for sponsorship is almost as important as your sales call. Divide your potential sponsors into relevant categories that will ensure you are talking to the right companies.

Generally, I suggest two key categories of potential sponsors. First, make a list of what you consider to be the absolute best fit for your company, your markets, your sanctioning body and your community. These are companies whose target markets include people who love your sport or entertainment genre. These are companies who you think should be your partners, that you might have some access to or that you'd like to get to know.

The second category could be companies that don't engage in significant sponsorship activities that you think need to be nudged in that direction because they have not thought about it yet. Later, you can try to run these companies through your sales cycle to see what you can do to bring them along to a better understanding of what you can do for them.

These two categories should give you enough companies that you can pursue for some time. Also, do some research about companies that you don't know about that could fit in these categories and put them on the list for further research and contacts.

Next, look locally to the area immediately adjacent to your office. This town benefits from your participation and there may be some fans among these companies that admire your efforts. Do your local prospecting by talking to people in the neighborhoods where you do business. These businesses may be willing to trade products and services in return for exposure and a little hospitality. Look through your local Business Directory or Yellow Pages. On the Internet, visit your local Chamber of Commerce web site and other local web sites and directories. You may find other companies here that are willing to trade product and services in return for affiliate level logo placement on your car, trailer, bus or equipment. Maintain a database of these companies and record all information you receive about these companies so you can be aware of opportunities. Your key for these companies is to tell them the exposure you receive locally can be exploited by them to gain product and service loyalty. You can also send business their way anytime you hear of someone needing their products and services. Make sure, if you offer this possibility, that you develop a business process to seek out these opportunities for your sponsor.

Next look at Regional companies that have a local flavor and pursue their regional markets aggressively. These companies love the support they gain from being involved in their regional markets and plan much of their marketing activities regionally.

Before you contact them, develop ideas on how you can

help them gain awareness in their region. Research their industry and find out where they sit compared to other companies. How often do you get in front of the public in their territories? Do their customer demographics match your fan demographics?

Do they compete in the marketplace against other sponsors already in your sport or activity? Why shouldn't they compete there in addition to competing in the marketplace? What kinds of things can you do to help them gain awareness that the other sponsors are not getting from their sponsorships? Know the answers to these questions and you will get a hearing.

Does your sanctioning body have a national following? Do you get in front of the public all over the country? Is national exposure a possibility for you? A national company can be a huge catch for you and put you on the map. Further, such companies have significant marketing budgets and have played the sponsorship game for years. They know the ins and outs and they expect you to know them as well. They want to sponsor teams and celebrities that put them on the map and they look for professionalism from their properties.

You should develop a database of potential sponsors and do your best to develop personal and business relationships with the management of these target companies. By developing an internal sponsor advocate within a company and keeping this person informed of important information regarding your activities, you lay the groundwork for future participation. Don't be afraid to schmooze and don't be stingy with the freebies. It may never pay off in sponsorship, but tips and information that these people give about their industry and other opportunities can be helpful. Sooner or later, they will deliver for you in some way. That is in the nature of "comps."

A key piece of information includes the latest revenue numbers for your target. You can find this information on websites such as Hoovers.com which lists most public companies and additional information such as who the key officials are, their responsibilities and job titles. The financial data gives you an idea if the company is even worth approaching. You want good revenues and growth over the last few years. You can use a multiplier (percentage) to identify how large their marketing budget is. For instance, you'll want to get a good grip on the average percentage of revenues that are spent on marketing. As you ask your questions try to identify how large their marketing budget is and compare that size, in terms of dollars, to their revenues. I've always used 10% as my guideline and if the resulting number is less than you are asking for your top level sponsorship package, you should decide if it is worth pursuing.

Another important piece of information that you should always be trying to get into your database about each company is the target's marketing goals. Acknowledge that the target's marketing plan is all about increasing sales. The target sponsor is thinking about this when he considers your proposal. His mental wheels spin with new ideas when you are hitting his hot buttons and he will yawn if you are not making the connection and sit up when you are. Therefore, it is imperative that you understand he is not interested in helping you; but in helping himself. This is as it should be. He is always thinking about increasing market share and he has given you his time and attention in the hope that you can help him achieve that. Is the company looking strictly for impressions or are they more interested in hospitality services that will enable them to close deals? Are they trying to drive customers to retail stores or give samples at events? Are they trying to attract web clicks and online orders or insurance premiums?

You should also learn whether they have a large marketing department or a small one. Large marketing departments tend to be highly segmented with a lot of people specializing only in small parts of the overall marketing program. One individual may be responsible for selecting new properties or events to sponsor while another may be involved with program activation and management. Are you even talking to the right person, a player with influence or someone who wants to make a name for him/herself by bringing in new ideas? Use every contact but make sure the contact is helping you get to the right person, not just playing for hospitality and freebies.

Most large companies have a well-defined marketing plan. Your goal is to become part of that plan. The marketing plan is a blueprint for corporate growth. It provides a roadmap for what will be done, who will do it and how it fits into the overall plan. The likelihood is that sport marketing and other sponsorships are already part of it. The question is how easily can your company fit into it and are you the best bet for achieving the sport or entertainment marketing part of the plan? Needless to say, if you know nothing about the goals defined in the marketing plan, you are rolling the dice when you present your proposal. Your internal advocate should be a great resource for you and you will be successful in convincing him/her of your viability if you ask the right questions.

One important detail you want to get from your advocate is key geographic marketing information. Are there important markets for this company where you compete or perform? Have you ever won or performed there? How popular are you in that market? What are those markets and how important are they for their marketing plans and strategies. What are they already doing in each of those markets? Consider how you can help strengthen their strategy for them and help them gain market share against a key competitor. This can be critical information to include in your sponsorship proposal.

In many cases, sponsors defer to agencies to help make sponsorship decisions. Make sure you research the relationship between a sponsor and the agency as well as how decisions are made.

In prospecting for sponsors, use technology to leverage your efforts as much as possible. A short introductory email is often much better received today than an introductory letter, particularly since emails can be easily deleted if they are not of interest. If you get a response, you may have made a big step toward getting your foot in the door.

A word of caution: even emails are better received if they are written like a letter, professional and formal. Always use "Mr." or "Mrs.," etc. when addressing the executive (at least until you get on a first name basis). Keep communications short but complete and "knowledge-based" rather than "salesie." This means you should provide usable information and data rather than sales pitches. Rather than saying, "We can help you get your message to the fans," provide information on how your sport, team or celebrity has helped promote products. Ask them to respond if they'd like to learn more. Use industry research and information and you will become part of the pipeline that the customer uses when making decisions…and you will be better received rather than deleted. Ensure that the subject line of the email promises usable information so it will be noticed and read. Finally, never spam or send unsolicited emails. Use only "published" email addresses and it is more appropriate to ask first if you can send some info by return email.

I've always believed that you should follow up every letter or email with a phone call. In today's business world, almost every phone is tied to voicemail and you will seldom get to the person anyway, but a voicemail can be a good opportunity to offer information, invitations and freebies. If they don't respond, you haven't hit the right chord and need more info. Ask around about the company.

When talking to the prospect, don't mistake the request for a proposal or literature as an indication of interest in your team. This request may merely be a way of getting rid of you and off the phone. Ask questions that will help you determine if they are really interested in finding new teams to sponsor. Ask them if they are interested in your sport or entertainment genre. Make sure you are talking to the decision maker. These additional questions will save you needless time and money.

Prospecting Tips
- Prospecting is all about qualifying the prospect and turning it into a viable lead that you can move into the Sponsorship Sales Cycle (see below). This means you bring the lead through the four phases of the sales cycle. Each of these phases is important and must be completed.

- It is important to determine if you have an experienced sponsor or a company that is interested in investigating the possibilities of using sponsorship to promote products and services – it is easy enough to approach companies that you know are involved in sponsorship, but there are many companies that would be interested if approached and sold on the idea – so the first question when qualifying a prospect is: "Has your company ever used sport or entertainment sponsorship in the past?" If yes, then you want to learn as much as you can about their experience. Was it good or did things happen that turned them off on the idea? If they've never sponsored before, you may have to skew your presentation toward convincing them of the benefits of sponsorship first before presenting your proposal. If they have sponsored before, ask them about their experience. Is there anything they didn't get out of it in the past that you can address?
- If you can determine the status of their sponsorship budget, you will also be able to qualify the prospect further. Are they already spent for the year? If so, when would be a good time to get back so they might be considered for next year's budget? If they have some money left in the budget, perhaps they can take a lower level sponsorship to test the waters and then come back next year when the next budget is being developed. Keep in mind, most companies want to spend less than what is in the budget, so try to come in under that amount – prep them by telling them that you'd like to work toward a long-term relationship and

use that test period as a way of getting your foot in the door.
- When you are doing your research, a good tool is Hoovers.com. This website has data on thousands of companies and it can give you valuable information on their revenues, management and much more. Generally, I look at their revenue numbers. If the company revenues divided by 10 are less or about the same as you are looking for, then they are not likely to be a good candidate.
- It is always helpful to know who you are competing against for a prospect's sponsorship dollars. By knowing this, you may be able to differentiate your company from the competition by learning about their weaknesses.
- Determine the buying time table. Does the prospect have an immediate need for sponsorship and promotions or are they looking far into the future – find out how far into the future their next "purchase period" is and try to get into the mix of their buying decision now.
- Try to measure the urgency of their need by asking when they will be making sponsorship buying decisions. If the prospect is vague on this issue, you may have someone who is along for the ride, hoping to get some freebies and hospitality but not really serious about sponsorship. If you suspect this, make sure you are talking to the decision maker and/or ask to meet the decision maker. With this approach, you will soon learn whether there is serious sponsorship intent or lack thereof. If the prospect can give you definite info

and appears to be on a schedule in terms of meeting dates, deadlines, etc., do your best to get into the mix and address as many of his/her specific needs as you can identify.

Phone Techniques

Good phone techniques will ensure that you sound professional and worth listening to. Here are some tips:

- Prepare a script to aid you in remembering what to say – practice it so you don't sound scripted
- Introduce yourself as a "high-level" manager of the race team – this gives you credibility and authority
- Have your sponsorship proposal, especially your sponsorship offerings and benefits, handy in the event you have to answer questions with more specificity
- Steer the customer toward a meeting rather than just a sponsorship proposal mailing – this will give you a better shot
- If you do send a proposal and cover letter, make sure you follow up within 2 days of their estimated receipt of the package so the prospect does not go stale
- Make a recording of you saying your script so you know how you sound and what you need to do to sound better
- Prepare a list of rebuttals to the most common objections – rebuttals can help you sound knowledgeable and prepared to sell – Here are a few rebuttal ideas to the most common objections:

Not Interested
- This objection is a brick wall when it comes to sponsorship. Respond that you have some excellent programs that can help them gain new business. Ask them if you can send them your business card and a letter that will provide some details on how you can help – prepare the groundwork by stating that your programs are inexpensive and designed to return to the sponsor more than the original investment. If this doesn't work, then thank them for their time and ask them to keep an eye out for you in the media.

Happy with their existing sponsorships
- Ask them if you can send them a list of sponsorship benefits with your team or company – tell them you are dedicated to giving your sponsors good return on investment and would be glad to talk about how you can help them – give them some food for thought and ask them to evaluate what their return is on their existing sponsorship – tell them you have given your past sponsors excellent returns and would be glad to talk to them about how you can do it so they have a way of comparing with their existing sponsorships – if you can get them to commit to this analysis, tell them you will call them back in a few weeks to see if they'd like to take it to the next level

Just send me literature
- o The above approach will work with this sponsor as well – just get into their mind the team's name – tell them to look out for you in the press and media as in the first objection and tell them you are dedicated to great services and return on investment – mention your top programs, logo impressions and hospitality or other services as a way to get the wheels spinning – go ahead and send them literature and make sure you let them know you are going to get back with them in that literature – make a follow up call and ask, not to give them a sponsorship proposal, but to sit down to see if you and he/she can brainstorm about ways to promote their company or products

No time to talk – call me later
- o Call him/her later – but make sure you do – and ask for that meeting to brainstorm about working out ways together to promote their company or products

Price is too high
- o Ask what price would be reasonable in their view – ask them if you can send them a list of benefits for that level - but don't turn them down unless they are completely unreasonable – more importantly, stick with the original price as the best value, the best way to gain significant exposure and new business – get your

foot in the door by selling the lower sponsorship and then leave the door open to the higher level sponsorship if you can deliver the results you say you can – perhaps they will buy the higher level sponsorship next year if you do a good job – if you can, get them to commit to meeting to discuss it further

- In your script, reduce your words to key points, bullet points that only say part of the message so you can sound more natural – make them easy to understand especially when communicating your sponsorship offerings
- Smile – they can hear it
- Use assumption which means assume the positive rather than the negative response – assumption of the positive is an art but if you learn to put it into your voice, it can make a big difference for you – assume you are going to get a "Yes" rather than sounding like you will get a "No"
- Match the person's mood and tone of voice with a similar tone of voice – that conveys that you are in the same frame of mind – it gets an automatic response – they will listen to you
- In a phone conversation like this, you usually have only the first ten seconds to make a good first impression – practice that first ten seconds until you are certain you are positive and to the point
- After every call, ask yourself what you liked about the call and what you can do differently to sound better on the next call

- Listen attentively to what the person on the other end of the line sounds like – listen to audible cues about how they are feeling, what they are thinking, whether there is real interest – you must avoid getting ahead of yourself – this is often called "Listen, then talk"
- Finally, your phone script can be an excellent talking guide when talking to potential sponsors in person, so if you do it well and you have a powerful tool for attracting sponsors

Sample Cold Call Phone Contact Script

Tip: Scripts are never designed to be read verbatim. You must present yourself with a conversational tone and not sound like you are reading. To help you with this we have taken the scripts below and created a list of bullet points for each one so you can sound more natural. It is also a good idea to practice your script with someone before you call so you will sound more polished. The more practice you have the better you will sound.

Also, it is best to find out as much as you can about the company you are calling before you make a cold call. Check the web site or call ahead for a copy of the annual report. The web site may have a section for companies seeking charitable contributions or sponsorships. Look it over carefully. If they publish their sponsorship proposal guidelines online, print it out and study it carefully. Also, look for the names, email addresses and phone numbers of people involved in marketing or sponsorship decisions. Record all this information on your client information sheet.

Script
Cold Call: You have never contacted the company before.

Good morning, my name is _____ with _____. I'm hoping you can help me. Can you direct me to the individual responsible for marketing or sponsorship programs (If you already know this person's name, just ask for him/her)? Would you mind telling me the name and title of the person I will talk to?

Once on phone:

Good morning, Mr/Ms _____. My name is _____ with _____. We presently have sponsorship opportunities available. I'm calling to learn about your sponsorship activities to see if we can help you with your marketing programs in these areas. (Do not ask this next question if you already know the answer) Does your company presently do any sport programs? (If "No") Would you mind if I send you some information about the potential benefits of sponsorship and a sponsorship proposal from my organization?

If you have researched the company, use this script:

Good morning, Mr/Ms _____. My name is _____ with _____. We presently have sponsorship opportunities that can help your company gain more exposure in our markets. I've been researching your sponsorship programs and wonder if you'd be open to looking over a sponsorship proposal from our organization. Do you have any openings in your budget for a new team? (If the answer is "No," ask: When would you be looking to make your sponsorship decisions for next year? (If he/she answers) Would you mind if I contact you sometime before then to pursue sponsorship then? (If he/she says "Ok," ask) When would be the best time for me to make that contact?

(Write down the person's response and any other information or interests in order to tailor your presentation to their needs) Before I do that, would it be possible to sit down with you for a few minutes next (specify day) _____ so I can learn a little about your company and tailor a presentation to your marketing goals? (Notice, even though this prospect is not interested in sponsoring you this year, you want to make a good first impression. That is why you are trying to schedule a meeting to get a jump on the following year. When the right time comes, you will be ready and he will know it. This will get your foot in the door and give you "top of mind" presence when the time comes to talk again. At your meeting, ask lots of questions, learn everything you can and write it down. Then ensure that he/she knows when you will be getting back with him for next year.

If he/she would prefer a different day or time to meet, make sure you write it down.

At this meeting, keep the following questions in mind – and make sure you listen and take good notes.

- Is facility signage a category of sponsorship you favor? If the answer is "No," find out why not and see if there is an opening to learning more about it for future consideration.
- Do you require exclusivity in your industry category from a sponsor? This means that they don't want another company in their industry among your sponsors. You will waste your time presenting a proposal if you already have such a sponsor.
- What is your primary goal in sponsorship and what do you expect your sponsored teams to include in their proposal?
- Do you require any audience statistical reporting, research or other sales activities at the track?
- Do you look for a certain percentage of the sponsorship investment to be spent by the team on enhancing the sponsorship?
- How much do you usually spend, in addition to the sponsorship investment, in leveraging the sponsorship and what would you like the team to do in return for this support? This can be measured in dollars or in a percentage of the cost of the sponsorship. Typically, a sponsor won't get their money's worth unless they spend an equal amount on the sponsorship.
- Can you give me some information about your core branding goals? What tag lines, images, icons, values and messages do you seek to promote through your sponsorships and how can the team aid you in

communicating them?

Now you are ready to plan for the next meeting and you've got lots of background information and he or she will remember that you took the time to learn about his company. It is a good idea, to maintain contact during the season, perhaps invite him/her and the family out to the track with free tickets and lunch. Ask him/her to bring the boss or anyone else he/she wants to have a good time at the track. Once there, let them bring up the idea of sponsorship in the future, let them see the value you bring and ensure that someone is there from the team to entertain them, a driver, wife, marketing person to make sure they have a good time, etc. Remember, you don't have to high pressure them. The fact that you offered the tickets and entertainment and bring the athlete/celebrity to the meetings means they had a good time and this is more important than asking them for a letter of intent. If the opportunity presents itself, go for it.

Sales Management

- Sales Management

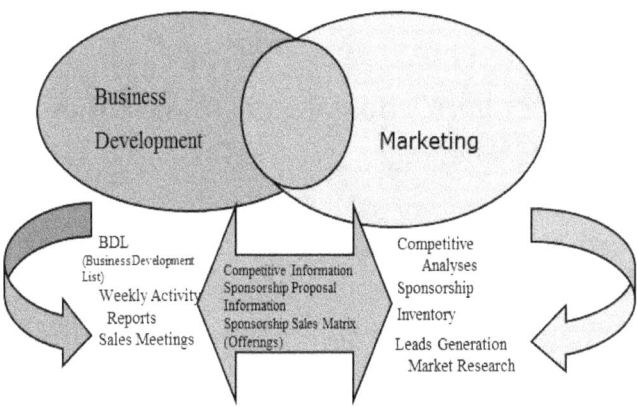

Marketing and Sales Processes

The Sales Process

In his book, SPIN Selling by Neil Rackham, the author defines the stages of a major sale.

SPIN Selling
SPIN Selling is the top-tier of sales methodology. In the case of sponsorship sales, it starts with the assumption that sponsorship is a major sale and that regular sales techniques such as pressure sales tactics will not work.

When you are attempting to work out a sponsorship arrangement with a target, the best approach is the consultative approach. This means you should approach your potential sponsor as a problem solver who wants to help solve marketing problems by bringing real solutions to his program. The SPIN selling model consists of the following:

S = Situation
P = Problem Statement
I = Implications
N = Need

To elaborate, here's how Rackham describes each stage in his book, SPIN Selling:

"1.   Situation Questions. At the start of the call, successful people tend to ask data-gathering questions about facts and background. Typical Situation Questions would be "How long have you had your present equipment?" or "Could you tell me about your company's growth plans?" Although Situation Questions have an important fact finding role, successful people don't overuse them because too many (questions) can bore or irritate the buyer. (Sometimes the best way to get your questions answered is to make a list of them and then see if you can find the answers from their website or from people you know who work there. A good Google lookup can often yield some amazing information.)

"2.   Problem Questions. Once sufficient information has been established about the buyer's situation, successful people tend to move to a second type of question. They ask, for example, "Is this operation difficult to perform?"

or "Are you worried about the quality you get from your old machine?" Questions like these, which we call Problem Questions, explore problems, difficulties, and dissatisfactions in areas where the seller's product can help. Inexperienced sales people generally don't ask enough Problem Questions which means they are often unable to help the potential customer solve real and pressing problems.

"3. Implication Questions. In smaller sales, sellers can be very successful if they just know how to ask good Situation and Problem Questions. In larger sales this is not enough; successful people need to ask a third type of question. This third type is more complex and sophisticated. It's called an Implication Question, and typical examples would be "How will this problem affect your future profitability?" or "What effect does this reject rate have on customer satisfaction?" Implication Questions take a customer problem and explore its effects or consequences. As we'll see, by asking Implication Questions successful people help the customer understand a problem's seriousness or urgency.

Implication Questions are particularly important in large sales, and even very experienced salespeople rarely ask them well…

"4. Need-payoff Questions. Finally, we found that very successful salespeople ask a fourth type of question during the Investigating stage. It's called a Need-payoff Question, and typical examples would be "Would it be useful to speed this operation by 10 percent?" or "If we could improve the quality of this operation, how would that help you?" Need-payoff Questions have several uses, as we'll see in Chapter 4. For now, perhaps the most important one is that they get the customer to tell you the benefits that your solution could offer. Need-payoff Questions have a very strong relationship to sales success. It's been common, in our studies, to find that top performers ask more than 10 times as many Need-payoff Questions per call as do average performers."[1] (Parentheses mine)

The SPIN Selling idea rejects the old "tried-and-untrue" sales techniques based upon frequent closing efforts. Before Rackham's analysis of selling techniques, as described in the book, it was assumed that selling success could be improved by more frequent "closing" efforts. Many books on selling, even today, are devoted to teaching sales people how to close using a variety of techniques that essentially place the buyer in a position where he must say, "Yes" or "No." In other words, closing techniques are high pressure sales tried on people that don't respond to high pressure closing techniques. Rackham learned that these closing techniques were actually not effective in the "big sale," that is, sales situations where the purchase involved a large expenditure for the company. In those situations, the buyer based the decision to purchase upon a more careful consideration of the quality of the products, services and

---

[1] SPIN Selling by Neil Rackham, McGraw-Hill, Page 17 http://amzn.to/2bkdTbb

follow-on support. *I* would say that, in the big sale, the decision to purchase is based upon the sponsor's acquisition of knowledge about the product or service and the decision to buy is not made until sufficient knowledge is obtained.

I believe that SPIN Selling is completely applicable to the selling of sponsorships. A sponsorship decision is, after all, a "big sale" and companies have for decades based their sponsorship associations upon careful consideration of the value given by the sponsored property they select for a long-term sponsorship relationship. If you want to be successful in selling sponsorship, you must know that:

- Sponsorship is a long-term proposition, a major investment for a company.
- Sponsorship decisions are dependent upon a long-range marketing strategy and the strategic objectives of the company. They are not made on a moment's thought.
- Sponsorship property selection takes time and deliberation on the part of the sponsor.
- Sponsors do not generally purchase on the basis of "closing techniques" but upon how successful you are at convincing them that you are a viable organization that will support their strategic plans over the long-term.
- TAKE YOUR TIME with the prospect. It is not necessary to get into a conflict with the customer about whether he will buy or not. It is not necessary to keep asking him to sponsor your team. What

works here is to reduce sales resistance by learning how to move the sales process forward toward shorter goals about which the prospect can agree.
- The better you are at moving a contact *forward* toward shorter-range goals that investigate potential opportunities, the better you will be at getting to that final decision.

This means that during your first contact you want to establish a relationship and a project that both of you can move through to investigate the opportunities you provide. This means you want to show them you are committed to advancing their goals by asking questions about how you can help; showing a willingness to work with them to develop a fit for you within their strategic marketing initiatives. It means that getting your foot in the door is a big part of the effort, but what you do once you get that foot in is the key to being asked to stay. Stop asking for sponsorship and start asking how you can help them reach their marketing goals. Once that dialogue starts, you will learn how to create a sponsorship relationship – and with practice, you'll learn how to get to this point faster.

SPIN Selling techniques can take the pressure out of selling. You don't have to worry about a successful sale every time you meet with a prospect; you don't have to worry about learning "how" to sell or learning how to ask the prospect to be your sponsor. You don't have to deal with the butterflies in your stomach. What you have to do is get better at moving the prospect forward by investigating (with the prospect) how you can work together. You have to build a relationship with the prospect that is enjoyable, relaxed and mutually beneficial to both of you.

There now, don't you feel better about selling sponsorship?

I suggest you follow these simple SPIN selling rules:

1. Consider yourself a problem solver and let the prospective sponsor know that you want to be educated about their marketing problems and goals. This means you want to identify the sponsor's SITUATION regarding their marketing needs and turn that situation into marketing PROBLEMS you can solve. By getting the prospect to talk to you about their marketing PROBLEMS, they are bringing you into their confidence and giving you an opportunity to present solutions that could result in sponsorship. They are asking you what you can do for them if they sponsor you.
2. By adequately convincing the sponsor that you understand the importance of those problems (the IMPLICATIONS) for their marketing goals, you can offer specific solutions to their sponsorship NEEDS. Keep in mind that the IMPLICATIONS that derive from their marketing problems may not be known to the potential sponsor. A good approach is to try to draw out those IMPLICATIONS in terms that allow you to present the solution. Rephrase the problems

in terms of IMPLICATIONS and see if the target responds positively. If so, you've got to have a solution that includes you. Strengthen your approach by turning those IMPLICATIONS to specific NEED-PAYOFFS that the prospect understands and offering your sponsorship solution and what you can do to provide that payoff.

If you've gotten this far, you've brought the target into the "Sponsorship Sales Cycle."

The Sponsorship Sales Cycle

- The Sponsorship Sales Cycle
    - The Selling Process

The Sponsorship Sales Cycle

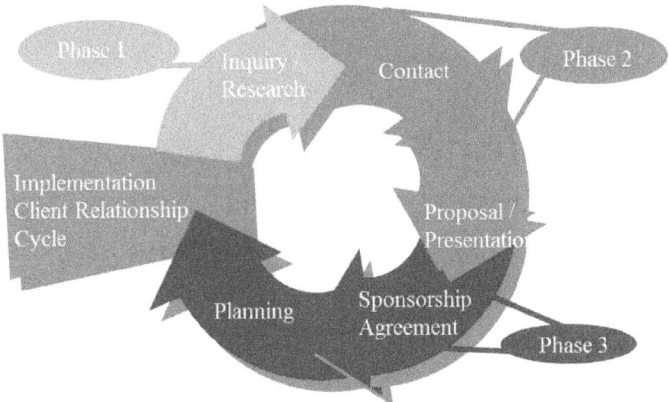

Below, I have provided some of the key points of the Sponsorship Sales Cycle. Although no sponsorship pursuit is the same, this cycle will give you some ideas on how to work your way through developing a sponsor by organizing the sales cycle into something you can manage. Use this cycle as a guide to tell you where you are in your relationship with a prospect or existing sponsor. It can help direct you to what you can do to enhance your relationship and keep the sponsor in your corner. Remember, this is a sales "cycle" and that means once you succeed in landing a sponsor, the cycle starts over – that is if you want to keep the sponsor.

Phase 1
- Inquiry/Research – learn all you can about the target sponsor, their corporate philosophy and past and present sponsorship activities. Develop a profile for the sponsor and ask critical questions that will enable you to know what you are talking about when you make your formal proposal. See "Introduction," "Target Profiling" and "Timing" above. Use the SPIN Selling approach.

Phase 2
- Contact – identify key players, become acquainted with them personally, ask them for assistance in presenting your proposal, ask them key questions about their future marketing plans. This person must become your advocate, your inside person who can help you knock down the barriers. Take your time with this person and don't move in for a quick kill — it'll never happen unless you are very lucky. Plan B, maybe even three years, ahead (don't tell them that). The key is to get an audience when the time is appropriate *for* the prospect.
- Get the audience – after all that schmoozing and preparation, it is time to make a proposal presentation. Don't leave a leaf unturned and make sure you put forth your absolute best foot. And be prepared to look at this first presentation as just the beginning of a process that may take a while. You may not fit their plans right now, so don't consider it a failure if you don't get the sponsorship agreement this time. Keep asking the SPIN questions and

prepare the ground for the future, even if it is a few years away.
- Make your presentation – If you can use a Powerpoint presentation and an overhead projector, do so. Convert your proposal to this format so they can think about the offer in the form of concise bullet points. Cover all the marketing angles and use this as a brainstorming session to get the prospect's "wheels" spinning with ideas. Be as open and creative as possible. If you have the ability to develop a Flash presentation, these software programs can create dynamic and flowing presentations that make Powerpoint look like the horse and buggy. But if you can't, Powerpoint will work. Always give the customer a paper version of the presentation to peruse and take with him/her. If you need help there, we can help at our website. To learn about our services, Go to http://www.documentservicesinternational.com.
- Persistence pays. If they have gotten this far, you can make the deal. Don't give up or get frustrated. Follow up every week or every few days, keep things moving forward. There is a saying in sales, the last one standing wins. Most major sales take between 3 to 10 follow ups, even 3 to 10 meetings. Just keep trying. Define your prospect as either "Hot" (very serious), "Warm" (may take a little nudging or more time) and "Cool" (interested but stalling or indecisive. If they are "Hot" call them every week, keep trying trial or incremental closes, take them to lunch, dinner, the race track...keep them interested. If they

are "Warm" keep in touch every other week or so. Feel them out, ask how you are doing, what needs to be done to give them the sponsorship benefits you offer. If they are "Cool" try to figure out how to make them "Hot" or just keep regular touch and see how things are going.
- If the prospect seems to be stalling, don't be afraid to ask for the cause of the delay. When is the decision to be made? Sometimes the final decision sits on a VP's desk for months while he mulls it over; knowing that a decision must be made. What can you do to help? Can you be there when the decision is made? If they say, call us back in January, call them at least 1 or 2 weeks sooner so you can determine if anything has changed before any competitors beat you to it.
- If you've gotten this far, congratulations. Now it is time to craft the basic sponsorship agreement. Make sure you take decent notes or have a staff member take notes for you. Bring your lawyers. Get a basic idea of what the sponsor wants and what he/she is expecting to pay. If you can have someone develop the preliminary sponsorship letter of intent while the sponsor is there, so much the better. If you can get him/her to sign it, even better.

Phase 3
- Now it is time to develop the sponsorship agreement. Keep in mind, the active sponsor may have an idea of how the agreement should read and may want to develop it for you based upon the ideas discussed in the meeting. If so, great...but make sure you study it

carefully, particularly regarding their understanding of what you have said you'd deliver and whether you can actually deliver it for the price. It is also a good idea to have your lawyer look over it before you sign the bottom line.
- Planning. Have a meeting with your staff and go over the agreement. Make sure everyone knows what his/her job will be. Have your "ducks in a row" because you want to make this work. Don't forget to congratulate everyone for their efforts in winning this sponsorship and, well…have a party too (Invite the sponsor).
- Signing and sponsor planning meeting. Once you are comfortable that the agreement is perfect and you are ready to sign and move forward, you need to sit down with the sponsor and plan the launch of the sponsorship relationship. Here you will go over your planned activities and communicate to the sponsor your planned diligence in making them a successful sponsor. Discuss announcing the sponsorship, press releases, etc. Oh, don't forget the check.

Plan and hold periodic review meetings with the sponsor to go over progress and success. This gives you a chance to correct any problems in plan implementation and keeps the sponsor in the loop. If you can develop data on impressions, product sales, promotional activities and venue performance, do so. This information is the best thing you can do to keep the wheels turning, so to speak, to position yourself and the sponsor for the end of the agreement and the beginning of a new, perhaps even more lucrative agreement.

Sponsorship Relationship Cycle

- The Sponsorship Relationship Cycle
  - The Relationship Process

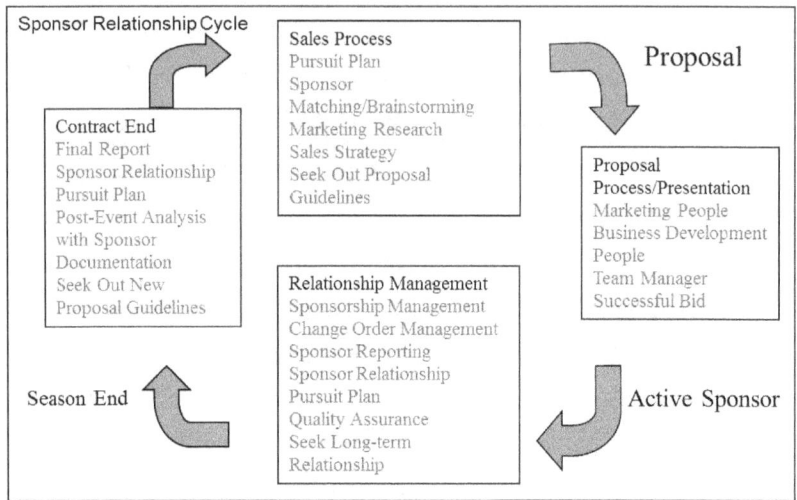

- Manage the sponsor. Schmooze, schmooze, schmooze. Call the sponsor after every event and review highlights of the event, results, marketing success, hospitality success, etc. Develop a sponsor newsletter and regular email reports – not just on your event results but marketing success.
- Now that you are a successful marketer of sponsorship and promotional packages, how about upgrading equipment? What you did well once, you can do well an unlimited number of times.
- Finally, you must evaluate your efforts on behalf of the sponsor. Develop effective reporting procedures so you can learn from your experiences and your

mistakes. Have frequent marketing and planning meetings. Develop an implementation plan for each event and evaluate your success so you can repeat that success next year. You must tweak your sponsorship promotional activities so you can get better as time moves forward.

Sample Sponsor Profile Data Sheet

Sponsor Profile Data Sheet		
Company Name	Industry	Internal Advocate
Address		Internal Advocate Title
Key Management		
Name		Title
Name		Title
Name		Title
Name		Title
Name		Title
Key Sponsorship Decision Maker		
Name		Title

Goals of the Sponsorship Activity   ☐ Increase Awareness ☐ Reinforce or Change Image ☐ Drive Retail Traffic   ☐ Display/Showcase Products ☐ Entertain Clients ☐ Other
Sponsor Profile Data Sheet – Page 2   **Ideas for Helping them in their Marketing Efforts**
Notes
Action Steps
Check Areas of Interest

- Preferred Supplier Status
- Naming Rights
- Official Product Status
- Single Race
- Primary Sponsor
- Secondary Sponsor
- Affiliate Sponsor
- In-car Camera Sponsorship
- Category exclusivity
- Licensing
- Endorsements
- Cross-promotional sponsorship

Sponsor Profile Data Sheet – Page 3

- Other (Describe Below)

Notes

Conclusion

This book covers all the key points that my experience tells me are critical. I seek to provide not only a top-level set of guidelines but also a foundational program that is intended to cover all essential points. If you have any suggestions and knowledge that can help in making this book more informational and helpful, don't hesitate to contact me at 1-317-881-3826.

Happy hunting.

Resources

About Document Services International

Document Services International specializes in the creation of high quality business documents including Business Plans, Sponsorship Proposals, Business Proposals, Internet Content, Ghost Writing, Resumes, Brochures and other business documents. We also specialize in graphic design and web design.

From our headquarters in Indianapolis, IN, we have created documents for business startups, athletes, professional and amateur sports teams, entertainment professionals, concert promoters and sponsors from all over the world.   Our document prices will help you make efficient use of your marketing dollars.

Business Plans and Sponsorship Proposals make up the bulk of our work. We have created hundreds of such documents to help our clients in their vital fund raising efforts. We are producing some of the best sponsorship proposals and business plans today.

DSI can also do non-exclusive sponsor search for teams running in national and international series.

DSI Sponsorship Proposal Service Packages for Sports Teams, Athletes and Entertainment Event Promoters

Your sponsorship proposal is your most important business document. It must be professionally done and clearly promote the value you bring to your potential sponsor's marketing plan. Your proposal must be attractive and to the point.

We can create your sponsorship proposal as a single item or as part of a Customized Service Package. Take a look at the menu below and decide on the services you'd like. Then give us a call to place your order: 1-317-881-3826.

DSI Sponsorship Proposal Writing Services take the worry out of your sponsor search by creating beautiful, stunning sponsorship proposals. Whether you are a marketing company, athlete, race team, sports team or entertainment manager, we can produce the finest quality proposal document at an affordable price. In addition, DSI gives you the option of purchasing additional services that update your proposal for specific sponsors or industries.

Below are the available packages:

Proposal Package #1 ($895.00)

This document is a stunning mix of graphics and content that will present your opportunity in the best light. We will present your sponsorship opportunities, signage locations and include plenty of benefits in the language that marketers want to hear - with a stress on their marketing goals and bottom line. Included is a stunning graphically rendered cover page to catch the potential sponsor's attention.

Additional options include:

Powerpoint proposal: Use the powerpoint for meetings with the client using audio visual equipment or as a print out. ($250.00)

Proposal Brief: A two-page brochure which summarizes your proposal offer. Use this package for mailings. First send the proposal brief to save on postage and printing, then follow up with a phone call to see which company would like to see the proposal. ($250.00)

Branding Document: This document is a graphical booklet that discusses an athlete or driver's positive traits as they are reflected in the eyes of the media, press, Internet and fans. ($300.00)

Web Design: 1-page website ($300.00) - FREE quote offered for additional pages.

Proposal Package #2: Sponsorship proposal document with added features. ($3,000.00)

This package includes Package number 1 (and any additional options you select) as well as the following benefits:

- 3-page website with domain name of your choice featuring your sponsorship proposal designed by our website designer
- SEO submission of website to over fifty search engines including Google
- Logo Car with sticker placements (if model available)
- Team/Athlete/Event Logo designed by our graphic designer
- Video/DVD for use on website (you must provide video footage)
- Business card and letterhead/envelope designs
- Digital .pdf versions of Mr. Villegas three-volume series, the Science of the Sponsor Search

Proposal Package #3: Stunning Madison Avenue style sponsorship proposal 17' X 14" booklet. This is what top race teams use when they approach the "big guys". You take this to a professional printer for stunning presentations that impress. ($10,000 Package includes:)

- Both .pdf (Adobe Acrobat) version of your document and .indd (InDesign) full-size format for mechanical printing are provided
- If necessary, we will collaborate with your printer to ensure the best quality printing of the document.

- Full 10-page website with domain name of your choice featuring your desired content
- SEO submission of website to over fifty search engines including Google
- Logo Car with sticker placements (if model available)
- Team/Athlete/Event Logo designed by our graphic designer
- Video/DVD for use on website (you must provide video footage)
- Sponsorship agreement sample documents for use in negotiating sponsorship contracts
- Business card and letterhead/envelope designs
- Digital .pdf versions of Mr. Villegas' three-volume series, the Science of the Sponsor Search

We are producing the absolute best sponsorship proposals anywhere. Considering the price, our service is even more outstanding. Our professional staff writer is experienced in creating business plans, proposals, PowerPoint presentations and other top level business documents. Our price includes a graphically appealing proposal document, PowerPoint presentation and sponsor proposal letter.

To get started on your Sponsorship Proposal today, call 317-881-3826. You can also email us at info@documentservicesinternational.com

www.documentservicesinternational.com

Books on Sport and Entertainment Sponsorship

Finding Sponsors
This book is written for anyone seeking sponsorship relationships in the sport and entertainment fields. The ideas and principles presented here are applicable to any company, sport team, entertainment company, marketing agency and charitable organization that uses corporate sponsorships to support its activities. http://amzn.to/2mflrja $3.49 Kindle $12.95 softcover

Finding Sponsors Forms Book
This "Forms Book is intended to provide samples of the forms mentioned in the book "Finding Sponsors for Sport and Entertainment".
http://amzn.to/2lxnTCF $2.99 Kindle $5.50 softcover

How to Write A Sponsorship Proposal
The goal of this booklet is to provide you with some basic guidelines on what to communicate in order to produce a winning sponsorship proposal.
http://amzn.to/2mPFnKS $2.99 Kindle $7.95 softcover

The Sport Sponsor Handbook
This book is written for companies that would like to explore the benefits of sport and entertainment sponsorship. It is the culmination of years of study, experience and success. http://amzn.to/2mB4K2x $4.49 Kindle $12.95 softcover

Hospitality Event Planning Handbook
How do you pull off a Hospitality Event for your biggest customers? You may not know how to start, what to do and how to ensure the event is a success. This book can help. http://amzn.to/2mxzpgy $7.95 softcover.

www.robertvillegas.com

www.ingramcontent.com/pod-product-compliance
Lightning Source LLC
Chambersburg PA
CBHW060406190526
45169CB00002B/769